HO
CHES

KAREN BUSH

THRESHOLD BOOKS

Published by Threshold Books,
The Kenilworth Press Limited,
661 Fulham Road, London SW6 5PZ

British Library Cataloguing in Publication Data
Bush, Karen
Horse chestnuts.
1. Livestock. Horses
I. Title
636.1

ISBN 1-872082-02-5

ILLUSTRATION CREDIT
pp. 3, 5, 13, 29, 31, 39, 41, 43, 45, 46
Dover Pictorial Archive Series

Printed in England by Biddles Ltd,
Guildford and King's Lynn

The common name 'horse chestnut' (Hippocastanaceae) originated in Turkey, where the nuts were fed to horses in the belief that they would cure broken wind.

The Earl of Pembroke, a distinguished military horseman of the mid-18th century, was horrified by some of the barbaric practices inflicted on cavalry horses of the day. He strongly opposed the docking of tails and the clipping of ears.

The Sybarites of Southern Italy in 450 BC trained their horses to dance to flute music, and it eventually led to their downfall. Their enemies, the people of Croton, played dance music on flutes as they advanced in battle. The Sybarite horses promptly went into their routine, depositing their riders and bringing about a Croton victory.

A Palomino gelding named 'Butterscotch' was actually taught to drive a motorcar by his owners. A red Lincoln Continental was specially converted for him. The vehicle had a top speed of 5 mph, and the fittings even included an equine seat belt.

King Henry VII (1457-1509) was not notable for his horsemanship. Thus for state occasions he prepared his horses by starving them first for 24 hours in order to induce a suitable state of docility.

The tissues of a mature horse consist of 60 to 70% water.

The backbones of Arabians differ from those of other breeds in that they possess fewer vertebrae. Often there are only 17 pairs of ribs instead of the more usual 18 or 19; 5 lumbar vertebrae instead of 6; and 16 tail vertebrae instead of 18.

When empty, the stomach of a 600kg horse is about 15cm in diameter – or about the size of a rugby ball.

Queen Elizabeth I (1533 - 1603) banned the sale of riding horses to Scotsmen.

Horseracing is one of the oldest of all sports. Races confined to horses of the same sex took place as early as 496 BC when a class called the 'Calpe' was run for mares only. Entries for the race had to be made thirty days before the event, and the riders were obliged to undergo a special course of training.

The first Olympic Games to include equestrian events was the 25th Olympiad in 680 BC, when both saddle-horse and chariot racing took place.

Castration of horses is said to have first been practised in England during the reign of King Henry VII.

King Athelstan (895 - 940 AD) received a present of 'running horses' from the King of France, and thereafter prohibited the export of any English horses except as royal gifts. He also set fixed sums of compensation for any injuries incurred by a borrowed horse: four pence for a small rub, eight pence if the 'skin be forced into the flesh', and sixteen pence if the 'flesh be forced to the bone'.

The quantity of water which a horse swallows each time it takes a gulp is approximately one third of a pint.

The broad-backed circus horses known as 'rosinbacks' gained their name from the practice of rubbing rosin on to their backs in order to provide a satisfactory surface for the feet of their riders.

The term 'Hobson's Choice' is derived from the goings-on of a 16th-century horse-dealer called Tobias Hobson. He would line up the horses which he had for sale and cunningly 'help' his customers to choose whichever animal he wanted them to buy.

The word 'canter' has its origins in the gait used by mediaeval pilgrims on their way to Canterbury in Kent when travelling along stretches of the downs.

An old English belief is that a fern known as 'moonwort' has the property of pulling off the shoes of any horse which passes over it.

From earliest times, horse shoes have been credited with various magical qualities and have been used as charms nailed up over doorways and on the masts of sailing ships. Nelson had one on HMS *Victory* at the Battle of Trafalgar in 1805.

Nailed with the points facing uppermost, a shoe supposedly brings luck to the inhabitants. Nailed the other way round it deters the evil eye.

During the reign of Richard the Lionheart, King of England from 1189 to 1199, over 50,000 horse shoes were made for use in the Crusades.

Horses do not possess a collarbone: it is too rigid a structure and would be unable to absorb the stresses created by locomotion.

The origins of dressage training can be traced back to the fourth and fifth centuries BC. The word 'dressage', however, was not used for describing the formal training of horse and rider until the early eighteenth century. It is derived from the French verb 'dresser' meaning 'to train, to adjust, to straighten out'.

Eighteenth-century state coaches were very heavy, and as well as a postillion, coachman and passengers, they were often accompanied by four to six grooms riding behind. This extra supply of manpower was frequently needed to help extricate the coach from mudholes on country roads.

The eighteenth-century English highwayman Dick Turpin did not accomplish the ride from London to York in one night, as is popularly thought. (It was supposedly to provide an alibi for a crime he had committed.) The feat was actually carried out by another highwayman of the time, 'Swiftnicks' Nevis, using several different mounts. [Turpin was eventually apprehended and hanged in York in 1739 – for horse stealing.]

Emperor Augustus (63 BC - 14 AD) encouraged horse traffic on Roman streets. Post stations were also built along the 46,000 mile road network of the Roman Empire. Couriers changed horses every fifteen miles, using the milestones set along the edges of the roads as mounting blocks.

Pony Express riders of the American West in the 1860s had to be 'young, skinny, wiry fellows, not over 18 years old, willing to risk death daily – orphans preferred'. On joining, riders had to swear not to 'get drunk, use profane language, ill-treat animals, or do anything incompatible with being a gentleman'.

Horses were selected for speed and endurance, and bought for high prices. They averaged a speed of 9 mph over 25-mile stages, with two minutes allowed for changing horses.

Each rider's round trip of 70 to 100 miles was covered twice a week, often through the territory of hostile Indian tribes. The service proved to be very expensive, and within 18 months had priced itself out of existence.

Genghis Khan (1167 - 1227) set up a very efficient postal courier system consisting of 10,000 postal stations. From 125 to 210 miles were covered during a day, with horses travelling at between 7 mph and 11 mph and being changed along the route.

Genghis died in 1127 as a result of a fall while hunting wild horses on the steppes. A herd suddenly appeared, causing his mount to shy in fright, and he was unseated and fatally injured.

Apelles, the Greek court painter to Alexander the Great (356 - 323 BC) was said to have painted mares who were so lifelike that stallions were deceived by them.

At the coronation of King George III in 1760 the Lord High Steward, Lord Talbot, was required to ride into Westminster Hall and up to the throne, where he was to swear allegiance to the sovereign before riding out again. Talbot, who rather fancied himself as a horseman, spent some time teaching his horse to back respectfully out of the royal presence. Unfortunately, Talbot's pride in his achievement plummeted rapidly: as the horse had learned his lesson only too well. To his rider's fury – and amidst much applause and hilarity from the onlookers – he also insisted on approaching the throne backwards.

As a young man, King Henry VIII (1491 - 1547) was an enthusiastic and accomplished horseman, but some of his ideas on the subject were less than successful. One remedy he tried on a nappy horse was to have a live hedgehog placed beneath the tail. He abandoned the experiment when he found it difficult to stop the frantic horse.

In 16th-century England a particularly intelligent horse called Marocco exhibited his talents to large and awestruck audiences. If a name was whispered in his ear, he was able to return a glove to its owner. He could also indicate the number of pence in a silver coin. Delighted with his animal's success, the owner took him to Rome to demonstrate his miraculous powers. Unfortunately, he was regarded less as miraculous than as the work of the Devil, and both he and his owner were burned at the stake for witchcraft.

A by-product of the farrier's trade during the eighteenth and nineteenth centuries was used horseshoe nails, which were employed in the manufacture of the barrels of high grade pistols. Collected by children from roads where traffic was heavy, the nails were eagerly bought by gunsmiths, melted down and fashioned into the required shape.

The Charge of the Light Brigade at Balaclava in the Crimea on 25 October 1854 lasted just twenty minutes. During that time, of the 673 horses in the charge 470 were killed, 42 wounded, and 43 had to be destroyed. Many of the survivors died later of cold and starvation.

During the Crusade of Richard the Lionheart in 1191 horses were difficult to replace, so any knight who found himself without a mount was reduced to the rank of foot soldier.

In 1251, a farrier named Walter le Brun was granted a piece of land in the Strand, London, on which to build a forge. The annual rent to the Exchequer consisted of six horse shoes and their nails.

Regional variations in horse shoes were almost responsible for the capture of Charles II of England (1630 - 1685) by the Roundheads after the Battle of Worcester. When he arrived at Lyme Regis, a smith was called to attend to the horses. Suddenly he turned to Charles, and asked: 'What manner of man are you whose horses have been shod in three different counties, and one of them Worcester?'

In England it is illegal to transport pigs and horses in the same vehicle: unless the horse is a racehorse and the pig is his stable companion.

The fashion for wearing top-boots was started in England during the seventeenth century when Cavaliers turned down the tops of their long riding boots in order to display the coloured linings.

Much of a mediaeval knight's attire was manufactured from horse hide – including the leather coat worn beneath chain mail, and parts of the shield and buckler. Much of the horse's own harness was also made from horse hide.

Bits were introduced in Mesopotamia around 2300 BC and were initially made from horn or bone. By 1400 BC the jointed snaffle had been invented and was in use throughout the Near East.

Although most American Indians proved to be expert horsemen, the first tribe to recognise the potential of horses and to take to riding were the Apache. Horses became of vital importance to their lifestyle. Buffalo were hunted and raids carried out from horseback; they washed their hair in horseblood, made tallow from horse fat and bowstrings from equine sinews.

The Appaloosa originated in China, but actually derived its name from the American Nez Percé tribe who bred them in the Palouse region of Oregon.

The horse is believed to have originated in Central Asia, and was first domesticated by Stone Age man – not for riding, but for flesh and milk.

According to the Roman historian Suetonius, the Emperor Nero (37 - 68 AD) never travelled unless accompanied by 1000 four-wheeled chariots drawn by mules whose feet were shod with silver. His wife Poppaea is reputed to have ordered that his favourite mules should be shod with gold.

The amount of blood in an adult horse is approximately one-eighteenth of its total body weight.

The equestrian statue of Marcus Aurelius in Rome only survived later Christian hostilities by being mistaken for the Emperor Constantine.

The small intestine of a horse is approximately 70 feet in length. Food passes through it at the rate of about 1 foot per minute.

The Roman Emperor Caligula (AD 12 - 41) owned a favourite stallion originally called 'Porcellus' (little pig). Later, when he began to win races, his name was changed to 'Incitatus' (swift speeding). He was given a marble stable with an ivory manger and gold bucket, a collar of precious stones, and trappings of purple cloth, and was appointed first a citizen of Rome and then a senator. He would probably have been made a consul – but Caligula was assassinated.

King Harold II of England almost had a mutiny on his hands when he attempted to make his Saxon troops fight on horseback against the Welsh. At the time, it was customary for them to ride to battle and then to dismount and fight on foot. At the Battle of Hastings in 1066 they fought against the Norman invaders almost entirely on foot, which probably led to their defeat.

The Scandinavian god Thor had a rather unusual steed: an eight-legged horse called Sleipnir.

A pronounced dimple in the neck or shoulder muscles of a horse is supposedly a sign of quality. The mark, called a 'Prophet's Thumbprint', supposedly arises from an incident which occurred when the prophet Mohammed (570 - 632 AD) released a herd of thirty thirsty horses to water as a test of their obedience.

At the last moment he called them back. Just five mares obeyed his call and returned to him, and these he kept. In recognition of their obedience he placed his thumb on the necks of each, leaving a mark.

During the early fifteenth century, Hungarian coaches were greatly admired for their lightness and comfortable ride, and it wasn't long before they were imitated throughout the rest of Europe. The first coach in England was in use in 1551. In 1564 Elizabeth I had a state coach built specially for her with four open sides – so that her subjects could gain a better view of her. In 1572 she made the journey from Warwick to London by coach, pulled by six of the biggest and strongest horses available. Travel in this manner cannot have been too luxurious: as a result she was unable to sit down for days!

A sport beloved of the Vikings was that of horsefighting, which continued in Norway and Iceland until as late as the 1600s. Stallions were led into a meadow and mares were tethered near by to arouse them. The stallions were then loosed in pairs – and the more a horse kicked and bit, the greater his owner's glory. A man equipped with a sturdy stick ran alongside each horse, to goad him if he began to falter. Although it was forbidden to use the stick on an opponent's animal, this rule was frequently disregarded.

The twelfth-century epic *Poema del Cid* immortalises not only the Spanish hero 'El Cid' (1040 - 1099) but also his horse Babieca. For twenty years Babieca, a grey Andalusian, was his mount on campaigns. The two met when the Cid's godfather promised to buy him a horse. He chose a particularly plain colt and the godfather exclaimed 'Babieca!', meaning 'stupid'. Thus the horse acquired its name.

El Cid died at Valencia whilst the Moors were besieging the city. Fatally wounded and knowing that news of his death would demoralise his men, he ordered that he be strapped into Babieca's saddle. Thus he led his men out of the city gates at exactly midnight. All were dressed in white, presenting a ghostly appearance. It was too much for the Moors. Crying out that the Cid had risen from the dead, they fled and were cut down by the pursuing Spaniards.

After this, Babieca went into retirement and was never ridden again. Two years later he died, and was buried beneath two elm trees outside the monastery of San Pedro de Cardena near Burgos.

The Spanish court painter Velasquez (1599 - 1660) noted that 'the Royal stud, through idleness, burst with fat in the mews'. The reason was that by law in Spain once a horse had been ridden by royalty it could never be ridden by a commoner.

The average horse secretes approximately 10 to 12 litres of saliva each day. It is essential to the digestive processes, and increases the volume of food during mastication by approximately three times – hence the feeding maxim 'Feed little and often'.

The first artist to make a deliberate study of equine anatomy was Leonardo da Vinci (1452 - 1519). Unfortunately, only a few of his accurate anatomical studies remain.

In a horse, the entrance to the stomach from the oesophagus is surrounded by a ring of muscle called the 'cardiac sphincter'. This prevents the regurgitation of food and also performs a useful function in that it prevents belching if the horse is forced to run from predators on a full stomach. However, the drawback is that should there be a blockage in the gut, the stomach will rupture from the build-up of internal gasses before the horse is physically able to be sick.

The Celtic goddess Epona was the patron saint of horses and mules, and especially of foals and in-foal mares. She was adopted by the Romans after the conquest of Gaul, and her image was placed over the barracks of the 'equites singulares', an imperial bodyguard of horse.

In Palestine the horse had been known since 1400 BC. However, because of the Law of Moses the keeping of horses was forbidden by Jews as being a form of idolatry. Any horse which they captured in battle was hamstrung and then killed.

King David of Israel (tenth century BC) was probably the first to disregard this law, and during the reign of his son Solomon large numbers of stables were built. It has been estimated that Solomon kept as many as 40,000 chariot horses and between 1200 and 2000 riding horses.

In India, horse sacrifice – 'Asvamedha' – was practised around 1100 BC. According to ancient Indian belief, mankind was descended from a mare, and thus horses were revered and deified. An especially fine stallion symbolizing the sun was selected each year and allowed to roam free, accompanied by one hundred mares and four hundred warriors. At the end of a year the unfortunate animal was strangled during a great public ceremony. By this act the ruler was supposed to gain prosperity and fertility, for himself, his successors and his country.

Placing a subject on horseback has long been favoured by sculptors as a means of adding an air of nobility, authority and military leadership. However, the equestrian statue of King George IV by Sir Francis Chantry earned the comment from art critics that 'the horse was the more attractive animal of the two'!

For years the sequence of movement of horses' legs at canter and gallop baffled artists, and they resorted to depicting them in a stylized 'rocking horse' gait.

The French artist Meissonier constructed a miniature railway so that he could ride on a trolley alongside a galloping horse in order to record its movements – unsuccessfully.

It was Edward Muybridge who eventually solved the problem. Born in England in 1830, he later emigrated to America and teamed up with Leland Stanford, a railway millionaire, to analyse the movements of a trotting horse. Using a number of cameras, the shutters of which were opened by tripwires activated by horses moving over them, he was able to produce a series of pictures showing the sequence of walk, trot and canter.

The hoof-wall is three times thicker at the toe than at the heel.

Horses employed for transport within the gunpowder works in the English Lake District were shod with brass or copper shoes. As the metal was non-ferrous, there was no danger of sparks. Horses were used until the closure of the works in the mid-1920s.

Probably the most important invention in the history of agriculture was the horse collar, devised by the Chinese. The breast harness previously in use impeded breathing, and the advent of the collar increased the horse's draught capacity by three or four times, enabling it to undertake heavier work, such as ploughing, as well as haulage.

The first horsedrawn firefighting service was instigated by Emperor Augustus in Rome in 21 BC. Six hundred men were enrolled. The equipment was loaded on to a 'currus' or tender, and rushed to the scene of the fire, while the firemen raced behind.

The word 'bridle' comes from the Old English 'bridel' or 'brigdel', derived from 'bregdan' meaning 'to pull'!

Superstition has it that nailing a horse shoe over the doorway of a suspected witch is a certain way of keeping her in.

The first international horse show was held in 1864, organized by the Royal Dublin Society. Two jumping classes designed to test hunters were included – the Wide Leap and the High Jump.

Horses were an indispensable part of a mediaeval knight's equipage – as necessary as his arms and armour – and great pride was taken in a war horse's breeding, training and accomplishments. A late-fifteenth-century writer described a good horse as possessing the boldness and hardiness of a man, the ease of movement of a woman, the short ears and good trot of a fox, the great eye of a hare, and the flat leg and good hoof of an ass.

When Alexander the Great died in 323 BC his funeral carriage was pulled by sixty-four mules, all shod with gold.

William the Conqueror met his end as a result of a riding accident. In 1086 he mounted an attack on Nantes in France and totally destroyed the town. Whilst riding through the falling embers of the burning buildings his horse shied, throwing him so hard against the pommel of his saddle that he ruptured his stomach. He subsequently died in great pain on 9 September of the same year.

One of the most famous tourist sights in Venice are the four bronze horses standing on the upper façade of the Basilica of San Marco. It is the only quadriga to have survived from classical times, and the four horses were originally harnessed to a chariot, which no longer exists.

A certain amount of controversy surrounds their origin; some scholars assign their workmanship to the Greeks, others to the Romans. It is thought that they were most likely cast during the 2nd century AD, and that the incised pupils of the eyes point to Roman origins.

Considering that each weighs 1700 lbs (770 kg) it is surprising that they have travelled so far. From adorning Trajan's Arch in Rome they were taken to Constantinople where they were mounted on the tower of the Hippodrome. Venice acquired them as trophies of war in 1204, and they remained lined up in front of the Basilica of San Marco until Napoleon removed them to Paris in 1797. After his defeat at Waterloo in 1815 the horses were returned to Venice, only being moved to Rome for safety during the two World Wars.

Following cleaning and restoration, it was decided to place the original horses on display in a small room in San Marco in 1977 to prevent any further damage from pollution. Four replicas have now taken their place on the façade of the Basilica.

In the 19th century there were many variations in the design of horse shoes. One innovation which has remained to the present day is the use of toe clips. First introduced by H. Hallen around 1825 to help prevent the shoes from twisting on the feet, they were originally used on draught horses and a little later on riding horses.

The standing martingale evolved in colonial India from the practice of fastening a turban cloth between girth and noseband on polo ponies to prevent them from raising their heads too high. The length was adjusted by tying knots in the cloth.

In 1598 there were complaints in London about the danger to pedestrians caused by coachmen who drove using reins and whip instead of having footmen to lead the horses.

Horse brasses are traditionally used as good luck amulets and to ward off the influence of evil spirits, but it is most likely that they originated from an eighteenth-century fashion among the nobility of exhibiting family crests or coats of arms on the harness of their carriage horses. Towards the end of the eighteenth century, waggoners began to emulate their superiors by fixing small brass decorations to blinkers and the corners of saddle pads. The trend caught on, and soon large numbers of decorative brasses were being produced.

Palominos were named after Juan de Palomino, who was presented with one by Hernando Cortés shortly after he landed in Mexico in 1519. The colour had been greatly favoured by Queen Isabella of Spain (1451 - 1504) who founded a stud for herself and her ladies: which led to the horses being nicknamed 'Isabellas'.

The rising trot originated in England during the 18th century. Road improvements made it possible for coach teams to travel at a good, smart trot, and postillions discovered that it was easier and less tiring to rise up and down than to remain sitting.

The infamous Becher's Brook on the Grand National Course at Aintree was so named in 1839 after a certain Captain Becher, a renowned steeplechase rider of the day. His horse hit the fence and deposited his jockey in the brook on the far side. On rising to the surface the Captain is reputed to have exclaimed that he didn't know that water tasted so vile when not mixed with brandy.

The nuns of the Order of St Clare of Havana in America raised the money to build a new chapel by breeding, training, exhibiting and selling miniature ponies.

One of the legends of the Third Crusade (1191) is that Saladin sent Richard I of England a fine charger as a present. Suspicious of such a gift, Richard ordered a groom whom he considered expendable to mount the horse first – whereupon it immediately bolted back to the Saracen camp with its rider. Saladin was so mortified that he sent Richard another horse, this time without a well-developed homing instinct.

The hackamore is not a modern concept. The name is derived from the Spanish 'la jaquima', a device which controls the horse through exerting pressure on the nose and jaw bones. It was invented by the Moors as part of a system of schooling, preparatory to using a bit.

Englishman James Fillis (c. 1850 - 1900) lived most of the time in France, but later became *ecuyer-en-chef* of the Cavalry School in Leningrad. He trained his horses to a degree of almost unnatural obedience. Among just a few of the movements which he taught them were passage to the rear, cantering backwards, and cantering both forwards and backwards on three legs.

The greatest age at which a mare has produced a healthy foal is 42 years. The greatest number of foals produced by one mare is 34.

Despite its tiny stature, the Falabella has a larger heart in proportion to its size than any other breed. It is the smallest horse in the world, and is named after the Falabella family who created it on their ranch in Buenos Aires by crossing small Thoroughbreds with Shetland ponies, and then interbreeding.

The heart of a mature horse weighs approximately 9lbs (4kg). Each heartbeat forces approximately 1/15th of the total blood contained in the body into the arteries.

Attila the Hun (400 - 453 AD) is credited with the invention of the stirrup, which gave his marauding hordes greater security in the saddle and an advantage over their stirrup-less adversaries in battle. The Huns were adept horsemen, said by their contemporaries to live on their horses, eating, drinking, and even sleeping whilst still in the saddle – disdaining to dismount even to answer the call of nature!

Foals have a higher temperature than mature horses.

In 126 BC the Emperor Wu of China was intrigued by reports of a breed of spirited 'heavenly horses' which 'sweated blood' and lived in the Ferghana Valley in Turkestan. Whether he was motivated by a desire to improve his cavalry, or whether for more selfish reasons he wanted the 'heavenly' horses for his own use, no one really knows. However, he eventually obtained 30 'superior' horses and 3000 of 'middling or lower quality', but at a horrific cost. Over a period of only three or four years the price paid consisted of several thousand human lives and 100,000 native horses.

The 'heavenly' horses of Ferghana Valley really did give the impression of 'sweating' blood. The condition was brought about by a parasite beneath the skin which caused bleeding when the horses were active during the summer months. The specks of blood mixed with sweat produced an unusual pink colour.

During the Crusades, replacing horses lost in battle was expensive: but it was nothing compared to the sheer difficulty in obtaining them. This fact was quickly realised by the Moslems, who took appropriate measures – as during one of Richard I's skirmishes against Saladin. When a party of Turks were surprised and surrounded they promptly hamstrung their horses in order to prevent them from being used by the Christians. The deliberate maiming or killing of horses was considered a crime far more heinous than any atrocities committed on prisoners.

The 'horse latitudes' are two subtropical high-pressure belts girdling the earth. They were so named by the crews of sailing ships during the sixteenth century, at the time of the Spanish conquest of South America. When ships were becalmed on voyages from Spain to Morocco and Brazil, the horses were thrown overboard to conserve water supplies.

Amongst the sixteen horses which Hernando Cortés took to America in 1519 were a pinto and a dark roan with white patches: the first multi-coloured horses on the continent. The Indians found them particularly attractive, believing that they possessed magical qualities which would make a warrior invincible in battle.

Cortés himself rode a black horse called 'El Morzillo'. During an expedition to Guatemala in 1524, the horse injured a foot and was left behind in the care of an Indian chief. In awe of El Morzillo the Indians housed him in a temple where garlanded maidens offered him choice fruits and dishes of chicken. Not surprisingly, he died, but was deified by the natives and a huge stone statue of him was carved – in a sitting position with forelegs outstretched. The statue was later discovered and destroyed by Spanish Franciscan missionaries in 1697.

The legend of centaurs – half man, half horse – is thought to have arisen when primitive early tribes first saw men mounted on horses and assumed that they were all one animal.

Frederick the Great (1712 - 1786) created one of the most efficient armies of modern times, establishing Prussia as a European power. On ascending the throne in 1740 he discovered that the cavalry had become thoroughly inefficient: the horses fat and unfit, and the men riding sloppily. He ordered field training to be carried out at speed, both individually and in formation. His cavalry commander, Seidlitz, tried to set an inspiring example to his soldiers by galloping between the turning arms of a windmill.

Frederick was the first military leader to introduce horse artillery to the battlefield, realising that as gunpowder grew more and more deadly the cavalry would become increasingly more vulnerable. Six-pounder guns drawn by six horses were able to keep up with the Prussian cavalry wherever they went, and the rest of Europe soon followed suit. The British equivalent, the Royal Horse Artillery, was founded in 1793 by the Third Duke of Richmond.

The early history of horse shoes is obscure. It is known that both Alexander the Great and Genghis Khan had rawhide boots tied to their horses' feet for negotiating rocky terrain, and that the first metal 'shoe' was used by the Romans. It consisted of a thin metal plate held in place by leather thongs. No one quite knows where and when the practice of nailing shoes into place started. The first specific reference to nailed shoes is contained in the *Tactica* of Leo IV (886 - 911 AD) where they are included among a list of essential items for cavalrymen.

The Assyrians were responsible for the invention of cavalry. Bas reliefs dating from the ninth century BC show paired cavalrymen, one of whom holds the reins of both horses whilst the other uses a bow. They soon discovered that it was possible to drop the reins and to rely on voice and body to direct the horse's movements, thus freeing both hands for wielding a bow.

The 'Parthian shot' was a tactic of Parthian archers during battle. The Parthians were superb horsemen, and dominated Southwest Asia from the second century BC until their empire was destroyed in the third century AD. A favourite ploy was to feign flight, allowing pursuers to get just within bowshot, when they would turn in the saddle and shoot arrows over the horse's tail: thus the phrase 'Parthian shot' has come to refer to a hostile remark made whilst departing.

King Henry VIII ordered that all stallions and mares failing to reach a height of 15hh and 13hh respectively, should be 'eradicated'. In an attempt to encourage better breeding and increased height, he also ordered that each nobleman should keep a stallion of at least 15hh.

These measures to produce larger and heavier mounts became necessary as mediaeval war horses were required to carry increasingly greater weights. By 1500 they had to carry anything up to 32 stones – when saddle, weapons, rider, and both human and equine armour were in place.

The white Lipizzaner horses of the Spanish Riding School of Vienna are in fact born black or dark brown in colour, only going grey, and finally white, as they grow older.

High grade white horsehair is used for the strings of fine violin bows.

The ancient Assyrians cut off the mane of a horse when its owner died, as a sign of mourning. Manes were normally left long, for the rider to hang on to when mounting. A hogged mane indicated that the horse's owner would never mount him again.

A 14th-century Hindu manual of horsemanship warns buyers of the many faults in conformation which should be avoided. Among the faults are: blue teeth, spotted testicles, hairy penis, effeminacy, horns on the head, possessing more than four legs, body odour, and a tendency to roam at night.

Possibly the first case of equine artificial insemination occurred in 1286, when a Bedouin impregnated his mare using a tuft of hair to transmit sperm from an Arab stallion whose owner had refused to allow him to be used for mating.

The quarter horse gained its name from being the fastest horse over a quarter mile distance. In early American colonial days it was impossible to lay out a proper racecourse, so races were held on short tracks, or more frequently, along town streets – hence the short distance.

Perhaps the first mechanical 'horse' was marketed in 1885 by The Western Mechanical Company in Exeter, England. Its advent was commended by medical authorities of the day, 'a good muscular action being given to the chest and lungs'. It was strongly recommended 'for invalids and all those of a weak bodily constitution' who were unable to avail themselves of the benefits of the real thing.

The 'Horseman's Word' was a secret charm, widely believed in many parts of Great Britain and Ireland to give those who knew it absolute control over any horse. It could only be learned during a secret initiation ceremony held at night and, once learned, the initiates had to swear never to reveal it. The brotherhood of the Horseman's Word was centred mainly around Aberdeenshire in Scotland, and was most active around the 1870s, although there was still a strong following until at least the 1930s.

The most famous early book on riding and stable management was written by Xenophon in 365 BC, and much of the advice still holds true today. But the first known treatise was written much earlier, in 1500 BC, by Kikkuli of Mittani, horsemaster to the Hittite kings. Inscribed on clay tablets, his *Hippological Hethica* deals with the management of chariot horses and preparation for racing.

Antoine de Pluvinel (1555 - 1620) tutored Louis XIII of France in the art of equitation. He tried to refine the aids so that they became as unnoticeable as possible, and he was a sympathetic teacher who did not believe in the use of a long whip or curb chain – something of a rarity in those days. He hardly ever resorted to the use of whip or spur – the latter being an aid which he considered 'a confession of failure'.

One hundred and fifty horses were reputed to have been killed during the filming of the notorious chariot race sequence in the 1926 film version of 'Ben Hur'.

The Morgan horses of today are descended from just one foundation sire. In 1791 a Vermont schoolmaster named Justin Morgan accepted a bay colt called 'Figure' as payment for a debt. The colt developed into a small horse, compact and robust, but with an elegance of carriage and a kind disposition. Despite his small stature – he stood just fourteen hands high – he proved so successful in weight-pulling and racing contests that he became in great demand as a sire. He proved to be remarkably prepotent, stamping all of his offspring with his own characteristics, and the breed was virtually established within his own lifetime. By the 1850s the Morgan was the most popular and widespread breed in America and had a profound influence on the development of light horses in the US.

The first horses ever to set foot on Australian soil were shipped from the Cape of Good Hope, South Africa, in 1788 with Governor Arthur Phillip's first batch of convict settlers. The horses were described as being a cross between the Arabian and the Barb of North Africa. They were not very prepossessing but were remarkably tough and hardy.

These qualities are still apparent in today's Australian stock horse, of which one of the most famous examples was Lucinda Green's eventer 'Regal Realm'.

A Palomino named 'Belvedere Forest King' owned by Bill and Louise Grieve of Canada is on record as possessing the longest tail in the world. Measured in 1980 it was found to be 22′ (6.7m) long.

The art of riding side-saddle has been known for more than 2,500 years. During mediaeval times, a type of side-saddle was developed in which the rider sat with both legs on either the near or off side, feet resting on a wooden board or 'planchette' attached to the saddle. However, maintaining control whilst seated like this was difficult, making it necessary for a servant to lead the horse.

At some time during the mid-sixteenth century the saddle evolved further when ladies discovered that they could be more secure and independent if they hooked a leg around the large horn of the saddle pommels in use at the time. A second pommel was subsequently added, followed towards the end of the eighteenth century by a third, or 'leaping head'. The advent of the leaping head at last enabled ladies to jump and to take to the hunting field.

A notable and accomplished side-saddle rider during the 1870s was the Empress Elizabeth of Austria, who hunted across the Shires of England. She took her own line across Leicestershire and schooled her own horses up to high school level in dressage. It was said that she far preferred the company of her horses to life at Court, and on occasions even stole away from formal functions in order to be with them.

The first travelling horsebox was devised by Lord George Bentinck who in 1836 transported his colt 'Elis' to Doncaster racecourse in England for the St Leger in a conveyance drawn by a team of draught horses. Generally, racehorses were walked to racecourses, sometimes travelling considerable distances.

Some individuals exhibit a remarkable affinity with and control over horses. An example was the American horse-tamer John S. Rarey, who visited England in 1858 and tamed a number of savage stallions during the two proceeding years. His powers have never satisfactorily been explained – on several occasions he was seen by witnesses to calm vicious horses merely by speaking to them.

One of his most famous challenges was in taming a savage and uncontrollable stallion called Cruiser, belonging to Lord Dorchester. The stallion had already killed three men, and could not be approached in safety, except by his keeper – who, even so, took the precaution of carrying a stout stick. As Rarey entered the horse's stable, the stallion immediately charged at him, but when only a few feet away he stopped as Rarey spoke a few words to him in a quiet voice. Trembling, he allowed Rarey to stroke and caress him: something that had never been achieved before.

Unfortunately, during all of Rarey's horse-taming exploits, no-one was ever close enough to hear exactly what he said.

Although called 'ponies', most polo ponies are in fact horses, standing between 15hh and 16hh. The game was originally played on ponies of around 12 or 13 hh, and the term has remained in use ever since.

A polo pony covers approximately 4½ miles during the course of each fifteen-minute chukka.

During the Middle Ages in Europe careful breeding resulted in the Great Horse, capable of carrying the weight of a fully armoured knight. Highly trained, the horses were known as 'destriers', from the Latin 'dextra' meaning right hand. One explanation for this is that the horse was led in hand from the right by a groom or squire when on the march. A more likely theory is that the name was acquired through the practice of teaching the horse always to lead with the right fore: so that if it had to swerve whilst jousting, it did so to the right, and not into the opposing horse.

The phrase 'getting on your high horse', still used today to indicate someone who seems disdainfully aloof, dates back to this period and to these horses. It refers to a knight's practice of mounting his destrier when about to do battle; the rest of the time he was more likely to ride a palfrey, which although a less chivalric animal was specifically bred to give a comfortable ride.

Before the advent of railways the constant traffic of horses pulling loads of coal inland invariably turned field tracks and dirt roads into impassable morasses during wet weather. A system of stone and log paved wagonways along which loads could be carried gradually evolved into 'permanent ways' built first with wooden and then with cast iron flanged rails. These could cope with heavier loads, and less horse power was required to pull them. In the early 1800s the rails were ready-made for experiments with steam locomotives.

It was originally intended that horses should work the Stockton and Darlington Railway in Yorkshire: the world's first public passenger-carrying service. However, the company's engineer, a certain George Stephenson, had other ideas, and when the line opened in 1825 it was his steam engine 'Locomotion' which was on the tracks. Despite the advent of the steam engine, horses were still used for many years to shunt railway carriages to and from sidings. The last railway horse in England was a brown gelding named Charlie who retired on 21 February 1967.

Poseidon, the mythological Greek god of the sea, was also known as 'Hippios', god of steeds, because he was reputed to have created the first horse, Pegasus. According to the same myths, the first man to mount a horse was Bellerophon, who tamed the winged Pegasus by placing a golden bridle on his head, but he later met his death when he tried to fly up to heaven. Angered, the gods sent a horse-fly which stung Pegasus on the rump, causing him to buck his master off.

INDEX